OUR VANISHING

OUR VANISHING

poems by

Frannie Lindsay

 RED HEN PRESS | *Pasadena, CA*

Book design and layout by Shaudee Lundquist

Library of Congress Cataloging-in-Publication Data

Lindsay, Frannie.
  [Poems. Selections]
  Our vanishing : poems / by Frannie Lindsay.—First Edition.
    pages cm
  ISBN 978-1-59709-534-1 (paperback : alk. paper)
  I. Title.
  PS3612.I533A6 2014
  811'.6—dc23

The National Endowment of the Arts, the Los Angeles County Arts Commission, the Los Angeles Department of Cultural Affairs, the Pasadena Arts and Culture Commission and the City of Pasadena Cultural Affairs Division, Sony Pictures Entertainment, and the Dwight Stuart Youth Fund partially support Red Hen Press.

First Edition
Published by Red Hen Press
www.redhen.org

Acknowledgements

The author gratefully acknowledges the journals where the following poems first appeared:

Antioch Review: "The Grail of Perfect Hunger" (previously titled "The Thin House"); *The Cape Rock*: "Lovers on the Red Line Train at Midday," "Prayer for the Homeless Man Who Cried When I Asked Him to Tell Me His Story"; *Crazyhorse*: "Upon Learning a Friend Is Now Terminal and Being Asked for Prayers"; *Field*: "Against Rapture," "Elegy for My Mother," "Watermark"; *Harvard Divinity Bulletin*: "Echo"; *The Journal*: "My Sister's Prom Gown," "To the Petermann Glacier"; *Linebreak*: "Artifact"; *Massachusetts Review*: "Mother's Bartók"; *Plume*: "Objects in Mirror Are Larger Than They Appear"; *Poet Lore*: "Old Dog Suckling"; *Prairie Schooner*: "Old Couple Swimming"; *Salamander*: "Photo Rescued from a Red Leatherette Scrapbook," "The Meek"; *Shenandoah*: "Cradle Song to One Who Is Afraid of the Dark"; *Tampa Review*: "45th High School Reunion"; *Valparaiso Review*: "In Praise of the Nearly Forgotten"; *The Yale Review*: "To the Muse after a Long Illness"

The titled sections in the long poem "Adoration at the End of Time" appeared individually in the following journals:

Breakwater Review: "The Clear Midnight"; *The Harvard Review*: "Adoration at the End of Time"; *Poet Lore*: "Prayer of a Prodigal during Holy Week"; *Salamander*: "Shepherds"

"The Gathered Stones" appeared in the anthology, *Women Write Resistance: Poets Resist Gender Violence* (Hyacinth Girl Press, 2013).

This book would never have come into being without the tireless forbearance and love of the Monday Night Group (Susan Nisenbaum Becker, Christine Tierney, Ann Killough, and Liz Moore) and the unending kindness and support of the Brookline Poetry Series, Denise Bergman, Magdalena Fosse, Joaquim-Francisco Coelho, and Marina Connelly. Thanks are due as well to Shaudee Lundquist for her tireless commitment to the final manuscript.

for Joaquim
beloved friend

Contents

OUR VANISHING

To the Muse after a Long Illness

1

And as the hour approaches, an old man
comes to my door—five-day beard, no socks,
topsiders worn at the heel to nothing—
to tell me he loves me.

So what say the pink and white petunias,
limp as rinsed lace from the rain
in their earthenware pot. *So what*

says the yellow and black baby snail
bustling along her homely millimeter
over the concrete step.

And the birds of the early evening
starting their practicing, little prodigies
on public school flutes: *so what.*

2

For then is there not the world
of the heart, the light that is more a darkness
from shining upon so much pitiful evil
and equally hapless good?

And has that light not yearned
for a simple roof to touch,

or the wondrously neutral tip of a ginkgo leaf
just for a minute?

3

For the very first time in my life,
I take a hand in mine, and it so happens
to be his,

4

and the ear keen to minimal singing
can still hear the tiger lilies'
lazy hallelujahs.

5

He had stopped being concerned
with dapper appearance: tweed coat, clean argyles
put away by his gentle wife.
Exhausted belt clutching itself for dear life
by the tightest loop
holding his dungarees up.

6

After he leaves for his early supper of porridge
I go back to my rocking chair
and the novel I left splayed open,

and read until I would have
stopped weeping.

7

Remember how the lankily rejoicing lilies
got louder at first, June after June,
then fainter, until by August
you had to make up words of your own
to sustain them. And then
they grew into the old hymn of stalks,
their flopped leaves like big Sunday frocks gone
out of fashion. Instead of the raucous orange
a stillness whose color only the wind could see.

8

But never, no never, ceased.

I

MABLE

Won't it be good when Mable can finally stop
hoisting her hips down the steps, taking forever
to squat by the rhododendron. How calm,
the chipped water dish minus her tongue,

and the mother skunk leading her glamorous darlings
unbarked at across the alley.
Dog for whom the coarsest weeds
will always part, here's your old leash,

where to—Grand Rapids? Tuscany? Reykjavík?
She stalls in the middle of River Street
locking her wobbly knees: she's got a bee
to watch. So I bend and whisper

as far as a voice can go into the dark
of her ear. I give her behind a push. Then
we mosey around the block, two aging ladies
out to remind each other how pretty they were.

In Praise of the Nearly Forgotten

This morning, after the many deliberate years it had taken
to give up waiting, a cardinal brilliant as pain at 2 a.m.
lit on the rail of my fire escape. One of these days
the entire backyard will go scarlet again
as if caught breaking its own green sacrament.
But for now the moon behind its last fair-weather cloud
is a woman alone stepping free of her robe
in a dormer window, her whole candid body
expecting her. One of these days

the gingkoes and motherly sycamores
will have to fade back to their inconsolable separateness.
I suppose I should praise the old, hallowed goings away.
But Lord make me grateful, too,
for the little, unfrightening shocks—
the dance step remembered, the flare of the shameless
hibiscus, the sweep of male along female,
the sudden gust picking up.

PHOTO RESCUED FROM A RED LEATHERETTE SCRAPBOOK

in memory of my sister

There you are, eleven, alive, dripping wet,
crouched on your favorite rock
after your one perfect jackknife off the float,

a girl with no periods yet,
unafflicted, draped in your mother's
modest bath towel, ears poking out

from between your splash-disheveled locks;
there is the Band-Aid peeling away
from the razor nick on your bony shin,

there are your hockey-stick feet,
and the small white flowers assembled
like children themselves around your toes,

and there is your gaze which God has yet
to enter, in which it has always been
summer, 1958

and a whole lake seems
to offer itself
to a girl who loves to swim.

My Sister's Prom Gown

If I thought you were listening now
I would tell you

the weeping cherry beside the porch
has come into itself

the way you came nervously down
from your bedroom

after I zipped you into all those billows
of pink chiffon for the junior prom,

I would reassure you again
that the seams of your nylon stockings
are straight,

though your ankles wobbled anyway
in those tall satin shoes,

though all of your hoop skirts and petticoats
scratched your waist

no matter how we arranged them

while you waited and waited for Charlie
to ring the bell, and let our father

snap your picture, even though
the smile that floats to this day over your face

appears not quite
ready, seems to be on its way

somewhere else, like the female cardinal
commonplace as a mouth without lipstick

who has just left
her rustling behind in this young tree.

MOTHER'S BARTÓK

Every November I am the same
second-grader waking up in the dark of the same

stern Monday to my mother's relentless Bartók,
the soap-sliver moon above

the garage, my over and over
wish she would lay down her fiddle,

cuffing my pillow over
my head, hands over my ears and then over

the ears of my bear,
afraid if I raise myself up from my bed to pee

that the nomad phrases will trail me
into the bathroom, as everywhere

normal squinting mothers
flick off their porch lights, as Dudley barks

the whole bruise-colored morning
into existence,

as the street sweeper chuffs up Rugby Road
like a world war, and all the while

mom playing the same coarse phrase of that same
coarse Romanian Dance: the dervish-like fifths

again and again, the ritual that keeps everything
under her housewifely spell.

What It Was Like Being a Tenth-Grader

Well I played snare drum in the marching band
and they handed us out blue uniforms
girls no different from boys
big fringed epaulets sliding around on top all our shoulders
baggy trousers one real fat gold stripe down each leg
Lord knew showing up every day in the same puny body
was nasty enough so I pegged the trousers
stitched the gold into oblivion
rode the bus in them like that to an away game
marched banging my turquoise spangly drum
onto the field under the lights
I could even sort of twirl my sticks
Doug who played halfback
still didn't know who I was legs and all
pants almost ripping and all
that was the night he never would

45th High School Reunion

It doesn't matter who's gearing up to run
for office in Maine or who has three grandkids
and just retired from being a dentist a lawyer
a hospital bookkeeper or if Maureen still drinks;
what matters

is that Tippy McHenry's father, sitting alone
in the St. Claire Nursing Home day room
after lunch, has a clean blanket over his knees,
his mind's one window letting a draft in now,
and that the early November light

still makes it through the torn shade
to lay its frail and dutiful beam across
the ugly linoleum. It matters that Tippy made sure
the family Steinway went with him,
and that she's asked his favorite nurse

to let him stay there after the trays are cleared;
and that his hands, although these days
they shake a bit like stippled leaves whose time
has almost come, still know more or less
what to do.

OLD COUPLE SWIMMING

And still they are helping each other
down to the lake they have always
dog-paddled in,

an old academic whose mind
is going, a hunched violinist over her head
in deafness,

still they are testing the water
one more time
to feel if anyone's going to miss them,

parking their sweaters
and Velcro-strapped shoes by the cattails, letting
the tepid shallows guide them

past the forgetful buoy
of evening sun and the dock's mossy boards
that ignore

their splashing; their stout, spotted hands
parting the water patiently now,
their inflatable wings

orange as poppies keeping them
lazily afloat, the black peace of weed floes
beneath them,

the trout and the emerald chill of their fins
paying no heed as the two of them
kick their white legs

as if they were asking each negligent wave
to rock them like fretful children, assuring them
all is well.

Unflattering Snapshot with
Dear Friends around a Deathbed

In the last picture anyone took of you, your smile
is already feeling its way off your face

like vanilla ice cream
on a paper plate outdoors in the middle of summer.

Outside an ugly white church a child in a too-hot coat
is gripping her blue giraffe
with an innocent vengeance.

Every last tree in the churchyard looks about to be
cut down.

Somewhere a woman who knows it is time to go
fashions a spit-curl out of what's left of her beauty.

Between them, you, getting affably spacey
with imminent nonexistence. Not a soul who loved you

has slept in months and here they all are
crowded around your maniacally sunlit bedside

wearing black T-shirts.
You are holding court with a cult of the guilty.
It is the season for squinting again.

The engraver has already blocked out the hyphen
after your birthdate onto the marker

the oak leaves need to be swept from;
that now and again a few disgruntled geese waddle across.

It's a God-awful shot of everyone.
They have probably all brought casseroles.

No one but you can look at the camera.

ELEGY FOR MY MOTHER

But I still have my river-mother
and all of her glittering fish,

my sycamore-mother who never is cold,

my star-white mother whose eyes
need no closing,

whose wind-stripped hands need not crochet,

whose dove-plain dress does not rip
on the drag of the gutter's wind,

whose kicked-off galoshes never lined up
with all the black pumps of the mothers
of Hillcrest Road,

my mother whose fiddle has two
curved hurts for its f-holes,

magnolia-mother shedding her petals of snow,
tearless November mother refusing soup,

leaving her wig on the steps
for the grackles to nest in,

my broad-boned mother, my corduroy
notre dame of the worn knees,

mother of sidestroke stillness
and loose knots,

my mother who blurs from the effort
of being remembered,

o homely, deliberate icon of lamps left on,

and I have set out a dish for her fingerbeams

II

Upon Learning a Friend Is Now
Terminal and Being Asked for Prayers

for F

So I send up another of my little gray balloons
asking the breeze or whatever to take it,
give it the oomph it needs, help it along here and there,
o that its string not catch on the scaffolding

outside the new museum, anything having to do
with a shopping mall, bridle of the chipped
green horse at the Altamont Fair, not even
the burned out S on the sign of the Rosebud Diner.

All this I ask pulling back the goldfish shower curtain,
stepping into the tub, turning the hot faucet down,
lathering up my hair, scrubbing the sleep grime off my face
with a washcloth I should have thrown into the laundry,

thinking it is a sin talking this way to God,
an absolute sin.

Girl and Dog Praying

for Kathrine Douthit

The Evening Prayer. A photograph from real life.
Copyright 1902 by C. B. Webster & Co., Boston

She and her nondescript elderly spaniel
are kneeling together, either because the good dog is a mimic

or seeks his young master's tired warmth
after another long afternoon in the snow

throwing and chasing a green rubber ball, and later
the same moist rag coaxing ice clumps free
from both their tumbling curls.

He doesn't know to whom she murmurs now, nor she
that her dog is a holy innocent,

each scuff of his weathered heart follows dutifully
the one before it. And neither knows

that the moon in the window watches them likewise;
the timid flame on the hurricane candle quivers

in both of their breaths, the featherbed yields
beneath the weight of elbow and paw, and

it doesn't matter that there is no Crucifix
over the little headboard, no Bible

beside the lamp, for this
is the prayer that beckons God in from the cold.

ARTIFACT

1

You came to put up with
the buxom peonies
Helga kept bringing.
First you asked them to stop
the prednisone, next the valium,
finally you waved away
even the laxatives
your bowel had so long given over to.
The white nun of morphine
tended you prayerlessly,
while all I could do
was spoon-feed you fewer
ice chips, tuck
the last gorgeous medicines
under your tongue.

2

After they come and take you,
the day is simple: the shade being raised,
room emptied, conversational
tones of voice in the hallway,
bathroom scrubbed echo-clean,
sky uninhabitably blue, no birds
moving across it, then one, then many,
while even the hospice Monday
grows busy with sheet-changing,

jokes getting told, time in the throes
of being ignored,
therapy dogs and friends
settling in for an hour or two,
hoping they'll know
when to go.

3

I have unpacked
the weeping figurine
that you made of yourself
years ago in the psych ward,
its berry-sized breasts, shoulders
the same tiny knuckles
as your shoulders, hair strands
scraped with the paper clip
they allowed you to use
under strict supervision.
Hands over the dove's egg
face, bent clay neck
the size of
my pinky.

To the Petermann Glacier

for Carol and Dick Toensing

as the sound of you clatters against
the sound of you

as you slink on your damaged axis
down each torn strand of latitude

      comes the blank midnight of summer

as you approach the silence beneath
the skirts of the jellyfish

      comes the coyote's glide over the boulevards

as the last oar lifts from the fleet of the white boats
as the beachgrass goes on witnessing

as the old man with no sorrow left
folds up the walls of his fishing hut

as he bequeaths his anchors and nets
to the soured new marsh

      comes the wildfire fingering
      the edge of the schoolyard

as the first of a thousand stones
grazes the raped woman's beautiful shoulder

as the ramshackle factories moss-naked asylums
doorknobs still draped with the gowns of ghosts
as all of the meadows cropless now
go on acre by wind-torn acre not knowing

that they await you
as only the face-painted sunshine awaits you
to scatter it over the shallows

> *come street festival sequins*
> *come unenforceable curfews*

> *come the relics the children*
> *should never have touched*

> *come the cries from the throats of the shadows*
> *of mothers*

> *comes the newly erected Cathedral of Zero*
> *with its pulpit tangled in sumac*

> *come deafness to fiddle and pennywhistle*
> *come all of the fallen honeybees*

as the lost gulls float inland scavenging sticks

as you lay down the calm heat of listening before
the great barrier requiem

WATERMARK

for CeCe Grady, 1961–2010

Your books swollen alive
in their tipped-over shelves,
the horrible water, shit-colored, lapping
your loveseat, sloshing over
the oven door's hinge, snatching
every Saturday you can remember
since 1983, every last one, and you and your cat
balanced at opposite ends of the last dry beam
of the bedroom floor
gaping at one another over this new
and deepening hopelessness,
what can be said? You got out,
more or less, the little boat made it across
the parking lot, your friends put you up,
you went back to work, told your usual
goofy jokes, but you and the rain
had come to know each other
the way one would know the face
of a man who had raped her in public,
in daylight, know it so well she begins
to become him, see him every time
her reflection grabs her and insists
with bullyish vehemence
that it belongs to someone else,
every broken umbrella
upside down in the trash is another

failed angel, and something less survivable
than this water that glistens because it is
only water, that has begun to end
the world, is rising in you, every day
you conceal the line of it as it grows higher,
go at it with sponges and rags and finally
the clothes off your back, and yet
every day more goes under,
how much more can the sturdiness
for which you are known
withstand, how long the appearances,
deadlines met, sister-in-law gone
out to dinner with, and the worst is when
the rain stops and the shameless sun
spreads out like a well-paid courtesan
over the garish new flowers.

Rain's Lullaby

Eight racing dogs float after hours
on moon-pulled legs

through the side door at the vet who wants to
get down to business

they have been losing
fractions of fractions of seconds

from fixable injuries

a two-year-old ninth is pregnant by accident

the kennel-hands who fed them this morning
now muzzle them up

although they are friendly
and wave the willow fronds of their tails

this one last time

some brindle some black as magnets and one
a rare tornado-gray called blue

the birthfacts tattooed in their ear-tucks
still easy to read

bowels still full

it is Friday the tavern will open early
hush to these things

no darling of mine must know

Objects in Mirror Are Larger than They Appear

That beautiful girl on a bicycle smoking a cigarette:
her library books are due back

and her boyfriend is starting to ask himself if
he ever loved her, although he knows she has tried so hard

to stop making those feathery cuts on her forearms. See how
the ashes of everything

slide into their easy disguise as sunlight. See how
her backpack zipper winks as if it can't keep a secret.

Death and envy are back on the loose! They are ducking behind
each bulkhead and pile of leaves in their falling-off clothes,

reaching limblessly out to the tips of all they are not
allowed to touch.

THE GRAIL OF PERFECT HUNGER

From self-knowledge thou wilt gain hatred of thine own fleshliness.
—Catherine of Siena, in a letter to Monna Alessa dei Saracini

1

Katie is trying to eat
and French-braiding the lavender
mane of the horse
she keeps at her place
on the dining room table
in the specter of so much
rice and meat
this calms her

2

we are licensed to
reach our arm into each of your
sleeves and socks
pass your uncapped lotions
among ourselves

to vote
on giving you back
permission after a week
to latch your door

you must at all times leave your singing voice
within earshot

the moon you refused is now the frozen orange
you have been given to grip
against this unbearable
convalescence

and while you are making
your umpteenth collage of pieces
of what you have been
allowed to keep
after you finish
your ten o'clock yogurt and pear

you will be called away (you knew
this was coming) on random
days of the week

3

o stillness at dawn o sleepwalking
groomless bride

o vanisher into the shadows of health
and the bosomy averageness
of lilacs

was it you

who left the pretend mother-
of-pearl brush on the bureau
next to mine the sweatshirt
slouched like a drive-by victim
over the chair back

the pills exhumed
during room checks
from under my mattress

was it you
who imagined the paper mirror
in which I find my face
now sketched by a practiced hand
for once with a decent pencil

who left
your cider-taste name
hidden under
my famished tongue
and the prayer glint still on my lips

4

no these are
my eyes my nose my mouth
o hussy of death o familiar
whose Goodwill sundress strap has fallen again

from the cliff of my shoulder
exposing that glare
of attempted breastlessness

no this is
my chin my jaw the very bones I wanted
broken and I had just the hammer
to do it

5

they give you a lovely journal
Japanese woodcut on rice paper
but you came with only
exact forbidden words
and so you record your spiritless
comings and goings until the dream
descends on you its great flap
of blank paper worse than the wings
of an angel gone insane
with pure sorrow for you
tearing his plumage out
feather by lackluster feather
and you scramble among
the shadows you know now
are of your own making
trying to find a pen you dig up
an ink-smudged toothbrush

mascara wand one of your mother's
knitting needles but never
that simplest of implements
this is recurrent and still
the book floods with
the panicked rending
of blank, blank pages

6

this is my body
as it will be from this day forward
done with shampoo
done with the good silk scarves
done saying *sure there is always*
that now isn't there
done agreeing done returning
your call done seeing
how easy that was

cleansed and sullied again
bog of lost arguments burial mound of birthdays

7

you had thirty minutes
to finish your sandwich and all
of your m&ms
we talked about this
now you have five

8

desert of questions to which the terrible answer
has always been yes
alley of known assailants
kindly shade tree
and the factual courage of lifting
the plum of my choice from the basket
that has always centered the sun
on my lover's kitchen table

9

welcome me now
as an old woman finally beautiful
to no one

up into my own
abounding absence
for I hear the fog freezes
before it allows itself
anywhere near the taut little throngs
of snow-green blueberries

For Marina

As the dead girl gives
her blue, blue eyes away,

so may the last of even
the morning glories finish

their daylight watch
from the chainlink's clench,

and the first snow remember
by touch each thing

the wind ever wanted
to teach it, then leave itself

alone with its white
and terrible candor,

missing nothing

CRADLE SONG TO ONE WHO IS AFRAID OF THE DARK

Here is the eager shadow a stairwell casts
when the oak wood boards for the steps
are still being sawed
Here is the solemn shadow of hair, not necessarily over a face
Here is a curtain's mannered shadow, behind which
a string quartet has just finished tuning
Here is the spangled shadow of one ginger candy against another
hidden deep in a Mason jar in a larder
And here are the crotchety shadows of dollars,
their smudged portraits of presidents
pinched in a money clip
Here are the nervous shadows of cards being shuffled
and of the white cigarettes and their smoke
Here is the sisterly shadow of water
the moment before it flows from its pitcher
onto a very old woman's bare shoulders
And the lone, true note of the shadow of a red-tailed hawk
the first night the sun sets early
And the choir of shadows of mangoes in starlight
over the open air market
Here may be the shadow of that which will end you
having outlived its last descriptor—
here may it always be, sweet child—and yet
the abiding shadows of all that shall keep you
are gathered around your meek blue cot;
they have shyly joined hands
for the saying of this

III

Adoration at the End of Time

Shepherds

for Irv Cummings

When chrome and din obscure the drear
of exile, and the donkey's coarse tail
flicks away the flies in tender boredom, when
the pregnant and beleaguered girl has no strength left
to brush the drenched curl off her brow
or wrap her thin blue shawl
more tightly,

when there is no water in the tin
to moisten her small cries, nor medicine, still
there are, this snowless, Middle Eastern dawn,
the outcasts scattered on the hillsides
laying chapped and shaking palms
with glorious uncertainty
upon their gray lambs' star-chilled heads

The Clear Midnight

Once more it comes down to a stable
that no one has used for years
filled tonight with shivering oxen, an unkempt mule
resting at last in the itchy, star-crusted hay

and the lightheaded girl propped up
against her teenage husband's arm, taking a sip
from the coarse-hewn bowl he holds to her mouth,
insisting to him that they fight to stay awake

until dawn, and that the beats of their hearts
are the footfalls of shepherds and Magi
approaching from disparate plains,
telling him riddles then singing to him

the peasant tune her own mother hummed
while she wove the cloak now stained with birthing blood
as the lips of the drowsy Baby
who never again will belong to her

fall away from her breast.

Innkeeper's Prayer

God please make of my heart a stable
where the hate-worn and drunken,

the brash of tongue,
the coarse of word and act

may rest the night,
star or not,

the breath of the hapless sow and llama
warming them; the poised and wary cat

keeping watch; and may the hay,
so itchily alive with mites, cradle

their shoulders that cannot bear the heft
of their last weathered belongings

one more mile;
Child, as the crows in the eaves

tuck their glistening heads, bring them
slumber enough, no light in their dreams

save the absence that, come dawn,
shall flood with Thee.

Prayer of a Prodigal During Holy Week

Would You know me if I showed up
centuries too late, missed
my bus, brought my washday mending,
hunched, embarrassed, at the back, one more

unhealable, squinting now and then
beyond the midtown traffic just to meet Your eyes
so I could say I did, as the same
vinegar-soaked clouds wrung out

their tannins on Your brow alone;
would You know how I had turned away,
sick with avarice, too many things
to do, impatient

with the silence I mistook as Yours,
my sullenness well-mannered as new shoes,
a polka-dotted dress, a flowered hat;
and when the hour came and then the minute

then the bitter, bitter instant
of Your taking leave, might we still
lock hearts as little children—one guiding
the reluctant other up

the steep and pathless hill, one sure,
one stumbling—toward its crest

as day broke and the young wind found
sweet thistles, pebble-gaunt

blackberries, doe and wobbly fawn
grazing in the Cross's generous shade.

ADORATION AT THE END OF TIME

Find the greenest hay and fill
the water trough, and tuck flames safe
within their lanterns so that He
may sleep, and still the sheep be guided
from the hillside dark. And place
a bench beside the manger where
exhausted wife may lean on husband's
solemn shoulder, and find rest.
Drape enough warm cloaks from nails
like those that one spring hence will pierce
His feet and palms, but not tonight;
tonight amid no song or feast
the barn cats gather, and the drab moths
startled free of their cocoons
swarm fretfully within the vague
halo's heat. Bring the strangers
in, and their unwieldy gifts.
Assemble all of these. And through
each rattling beam, let the wind
give likewise of its chill. Outside,
leave again the orphaned star.

IV

ECHO

When at last I can let the waves,
so tired from their pilgrimage,

nuzzle the toes of my boots
while I think up another

lie about God
to toss across Lake Dunmore,

I find my peace knowing
a gustful of starlings will carry it back

a little at a time,
at their leisure,

in marigold-yellow beaks,
letting the shreds of the words

that once made it into the old,
harsh prayers

be their new and adequate
nest parts.

Heart Dog

I can still step outdoors
before sleep, start joining together
the farthest, most
egoless stars, and hope
this time to get you right

your eyes moist again with joy
black glint of your nose
chin before it lost
its handsome and steep definition
hillock of sternum

bright bandanna
granny-knotted around your neck
your legs' white feathers
dancing with lust
at the scent of a liver scrap

if I stand far enough away
to finish making
my personal constellation
tail's haphazard corkscrew comical paws
lovely menacing teeth

then I can come lay me down
on the mound alive with your rest
as it swells in spring

and sinks again
in the summer drought

as if the ring of carefully
chosen stones
blossomed each year then wilted
back into their heft

as if you had taken a breath by reflex
to comfort the earth

How to Find Words for an Elegy

They have always startled too easily—
where the feral befriend
the coldest shadows and lake currents,
these, the wilder still
evading existence itself,

cannot linger here—leave them
an amphitheatre of empty chairs
where the long summer concerts were—
on this the last warm day
of November, know

the squirrels may rush about more scratchily
and the slow geese lug themselves
over the silvered air.
Ask the dimming warmth about
something else. Or sit down

in the chair farthest back
where the untroubled whiteness knows
you have nowhere for now
to go—and lift your coat lapels.
Ask the dimming warmth about this.

OLD DOG SUCKLING

You who were taken too soon
from the carton of towels and newspaper

after the brood bitch had finally fallen
asleep herself, off-guard for an hour

as you let your birth-blue eyes flop shut
as the breeder unfastened the milk-flaked hinge of your lips

and placed you in a stranger's freezing backseat
to be driven over the unmarked roads in a blizzard

later to wake in a cage that shone
with the all-night hunger of so many others,

now your old tongue clucks the same as it did
in that farmhouse kitchen where you were whelped,

you with nothing left to dream but your last
here-on-earthness, thank you

for leaving your dust-common name as the password
to every lock that opened my door

that late rainy night when the heat went, then all of the pipes
went numb, and I knew

I had lived too many insubstantial human years,
and there you stood.

Against Rapture

> *It. Is. Going. To. Happen.*
> —Harold Camping

Gradually things began to appear in the house
that belonged to the risen-away: dahlia brooch
on the lapel of the blouse she never wore,

pebbly bath soap damp with the scent
of a woodfitter's palms. Scraps of the red
that had never been torn into cardinals.

From her fire escape she could still
see the non-wing of heat lightning
grazing its chosen. Gone

were their rumpled picnic blankets, nary
a crumb in the brambles. Gone
their guitars and their little plump hymnals.

From the outskirts came reports
that even the slowest dancing had stopped.
Still, she took up her hair brush

and worked an errant tangle loose.
She leaned back on her pillow. Imagined
the downpour of valuables,

all that scared starlight. Noticed
the tepid moon failing to warm itself
in the old, stern hearth of the birch ribs.

Noticed the nightstand needed
a decent dusting. Noticed
how grateful she was for that, for dust.

22 May, 2011

13 Year Old Dog

Now old friend you ask nothing

accept these cradling arms that will not let you
stumble again on the tall tall steps

this rice gruel fed from a steadied hand

accept rest from this bed furrowed deep
with the years of your circling

and freedom from this collar slipped past
your chafed throat and lopsided ears
clinking once as it flops on its hook and is still

this slow walk over snapped thistles
into your beyondlessness where I am not welcome

this water from the crusted home tap
this one last time before you begin to hear

the clearest of springs stroking over and over
the brows of the rocks

The Meek

The crickets of late September
keep nothing
except the leftover white

of the workaday clover between
the garages abutting
Berwick Street;

the white certainty that the clematis
has curled back over the rec center's
chain-link fence

like the veil over a pillbox hat,
but vanilla
you have to think about;

and all the bright nights dwindling
simply up
to the steady amen

their calm wings know;
little *kyrie* of the chanting
starlight.

ROBERT

His spine is wrecked but he keeps showing up
to sell the homeless magazine the Baptist church puts out

he's still outside the bank's main branch but
he looks worse

the cup he's used all month the box-flap sign
that says *My name is Robert*

have AIDS going blind
the same girl jones-ing keeps him up all night

and lately he is listing like a ship that can't
take on more water

paintless prow heavy with barnacles mainsail torn
drifting into some old claptrap beach where no one but

the seagrass notices the tide
and all the chipped shells pretty as these

Friday morning women on their way
to work

The Girl I Am Afraid of Lays Her Head on My Shoulder on the 73 Bus

Your Red Sox bomber jacket stinks a little now,
your meds not working right (that twitch,
that holler at nothing), the Velcroed shoes,
but I would take you to the zoo,
steady you behind the railing at the pit

in which the dangerous apes
are playing with old clothes, making
dowdy outfits and then stripping
naked, covering their genitals
like adolescents in the shower after gym,

then aiming their stuffed hedgehog straight
into our hands, and beckoning with the scowl
they've polished in the mirror hung from a branch,
with hooked and waggling index fingers,
to be nice, and toss it back.

LOVERS ON THE RED LINE TRAIN AT MIDDAY

under the river no boats are out on

his chest against your plaid sleeve

your unwashable face
peony the aphids have finished with

how he looks on you

your heavy glasses
your big tearless patience

To a Homeless Woman Found Dead on Boston Common

your last hair strands taken away
for nest-making—

huge hem stitches on an old dress—

the wind across the Public Garden always knew
you were pretty—

come sit, the rain has let itself stop
my umbrella has nothing to do

but save a place
on the bench grown warm with your absence—

some day even your death will be gone

and the bag of bread you left me
to feed the dull sparrows

and my snow-stained jacket
around your shoulders—

PRAYER FOR THE 110th FLOOR

Lord of the morning be in the breeze
as it lifts again the wisp of hair
from the falling man's brow
as his orange shirttail comes untucked
and his life floats up
be in the ease of his one bent knee
and the thinnest altitude empty of all but the day
that has not yet been given its soul
be in the grief of the asphalt with no arms to open
and with the grass
the coarse and the silken tufts of it
as they are trespassed against
be with the ocean that must go on folding its only white
be in the sorrowless panting of dogs and in their fatigue
in the tourniquets unguents and spring water
be on the cheeks that were kissed
on the porches where those who kissed
did not come home
be with the eyes that watched
the glistening river go black in a single wing-hush
be with the sun yes be with the innocent sun
that touched the credenzas monitors paperweights
finding none of its usual answers
be the leisurely rain's descent where no stairs are
be with the dust in the oxblood shoes still laced
in the red of the broken-off heel the memos and pencils
be in the mug that did not chip

in the descant sifting across the hymn of the names
that morning that gorgeous morning
be now with this wrong-side blue

PRAYER FOR THE HOMELESS MAN WHO
CRIED WHEN I ASKED HIM TO TELL ME HIS STORY

Until the ocean's last supple coral knows me again
as its sister

until I have received the Host in a dirt-floored church

until the woman whose baldness frightened me once
whirls me scarflessly into her wild peace

and each petal of ash from the rubbish fire that warmed
the vagabond's hands
is lovelier than an orchid's laze

until I abandon the stream bank knowing
no family of cider-bright foxes will crouch to drink
if I stay

Lord make me one on whose shoulders
each harsh and innocent spear of the sun
weeps freely down

THE GATHERED STONES

after The Stoning of Soraya M.

1

This is what happens: the village boys who are old enough
set out with the canvas sacks
their fathers have strapped to their shoulders
to gather the sharpest stones, the desert morning
lush with marketplace poppies and marigolds
standing in buckets beside the gates of the rich,
the bleating and peaceable shitting of goats on the clovered hills.

2

And this: the accused alone in her mother's room
getting ready as slowly as possible, dressing herself in white,
a white lace scarf to fit under
her chador, which must be black;

it is not lost on her, the irony of how like her wedding this is
while she brushes her silken hair and pinches the last pearl button
through its brocade, and sings a prayer verse
to keep herself well-distracted

3

and the stones go on filling the children's sacks,
first a few rolled between small fingers, inspected,
found pleasing to God,
then all they can carry, jagged or not, their burdens becoming
too heavy or not . . .

4

She still could escape: the cypress motions to her
outside the tiny back window, but she has been schooled
in honor, so she calls her daughters in and gives one
her locket, one the ring her grandmother gave her

5

and her tethered camel stares at nothing . . .

6

The men—her neighbors, the widowed mechanic,
her younger brother, her teenaged sons—are clapping
pairs of stones together in rhythm
like shuffling boots; the jesters her husband has hired for later
are painting their faces;

her father has finished digging the trench
in which will stand her living ankles kneecaps pelvic cradle
before the proceedings begin
and remain standing up in the earth
unhurt

long after her back snaps

7

may the doves forever pummel the skies of heaven

as she gathers the gauzy poppies safely into her basket
for the table at home, at evening

8

and no poem comes of this

STILL LIFE WITH MORNING AND DOG

I awaken and nothing has died

the dog is upside down beside me
on the gritty comforter

white chest as if he has rolled
in October frost

lah-di-dah fronds of his waving legs

lolling and affable penis

black dirt stars buried just beneath
his rib-skin's vellum

his outbreath's breeze making me think
the word *willow*

one death-sequin in each
midnight eye as he turns thirteen

slowed heart keeping decent time
as I raise myself up on one elbow

scratch the startling, girly pink
of his nearest ear and say *walk?*

and he tips right-side-up
and his feet graze the floor before mine

so I follow him
down the boot-weary stairs

so he can finish a little more of his
griefless living

Photo by Sonya Highfield

Frannie Lindsay's previous volumes of poetry are *Mayweed* (The Word Works, 2010), *Lamb* (Perugia, 2006), and *Where She Always Was* (Utah State University Press, 2005). Her awards include the Washington Prize, the Perugia Award, the May Swenson Award, and *The Missouri Review* Prize. Her work has been featured in Ted Kooser's column "American Life in Poetry," and on *Writer's Almanac* and *Poetry Daily*. She has held fellowships from the National Endowment for the Arts and the Massachusetts Cultural Council, and has received several Pushcart nominations. She is a classical pianist and lives in Belmont, Massachusetts.